BECOME THE BEST YOU

About the Author

Reneé Davis is a happily married thirty-something mum of three, on a mission to ensure her kids have a better start to life than the one she had. When Reneé isn't writing books, or blogging at 'Mummy Tries', she can be found in her kitchen cooking up a storm. She daydreams of living in an eco house by the sea one day.

Dedication

This book is dedicated to my beautiful family; Andy, Polly, Clara and Freddy. Without you, I am nothing.

RENEÉ DAVIS

BECOME THE BEST YOU

*Make Peace with the Past
and Break the Cycle of Dysfunction*

AUSTIN MACAULEY
PUBLISHERS LTD.

Previously published on CreateSpace Independent Publishing Platform, 2014.

To find out more about the author visit her blog:
http://mummytries.com

A CIP catalogue record for this title is available from the British Library.

ISBN 9781785547058 (paperback)

www.austinmacauley.com

First Published (2015)

Austin Macauley Publishers Ltd.
25 Canada Square
Canary Wharf
London
E14 5LQ

Printed and bound in Great Britain

Contents

Introduction

WHY SHOULD YOU READ THIS BOOK?

THERE ARE many self-help books out there telling you
how to think, what to wear and how to behave. Qualified
professionals are desperate to give you their views on
any subject matter you require guidance on. What's so
special about me? I'm just a regular person. I don't have
letters after my name or a rags to riches story, so why
should you bother reading this book?

After having a dysfunctional childhood, and self-
destructive young adulthood, I broke away from my past
and created a much brighter future. Rather than just
talk about my children never having to experience what
I went through myself (like my parents did) I worked
damn hard to ensure it was the case. Throughout this
book I will share personal stories from my life and
insights on how I overcame the many obstacles I have
faced over the years.

I'll tell you how I broke the cycle of dysfunction,
and hopefully it will inspire you to go off and do the

same. Getting past my past wasn't easy, but it wasn't impossible. I promise not to talk about things that I have no personal experience of, and I won't pretend to have all the answers. But I might just have the ones you are looking for.

If you can identify with this list of demons I had to conquer, this book is for you!

- Raised by parents who had dysfunctional childhoods and subsequently had one myself

- Moved house lots and went to many schools

- Suffered bullying in several schools

- Suffered sexual abuse as a child

- Left home at a very young age after not finishing school

- Struggled with depression

- Got into a lot of debt

- Had very little self-respect

- Used to sleep around

- Abused drugs and alcohol

- Put myself into unnecessary, dangerous situations

What do I hope you will achieve by reading this book?

- The ability to make peace with your past
- The ability to look in the mirror and like what you see
- The ability to find your inner strength and start respecting yourself
- The courage to re-define the rules of relationships that have become toxic
- The courage to cut ties with people who make you miserable
- The courage to break the cycle, keep it broken and become the best you

What this book doesn't do

- Use overly complicated words or examples that are difficult to understand
- Go into minute detail telling you exactly what to do
- Patronise you and assume that you aren't capable of turning your life around

Chapter One

THE CYCLE OF DYSFUNCTION

"Life is too ironic to fully understand. It takes sadness to know what happiness is, noise to appreciate silence and absence to value presence." Buddha

Question: **What is the cycle of dysfunction?**

Answer: **A negative pattern of behaviour passed on from parent to child, which will continue indefinitely unless the person at the end of the cycle actively breaks it.**

MY MOTHER had a rotten childhood. Her father was killed in a road accident when she was small. He left behind my pregnant grandma who was carrying their sixth baby, along with five kids aged between one and ten. They were living in the United States at the time and she came back to London where she raised her family alone. She worked six days a week to provide a roof over their heads and food on the table, yet her kids all resented her for it. They would have preferred to have had a mum who was home more, but she thought she was doing the best thing by working. While Grandma grieved for her husband and threw herself into her job, the six of them were largely left to their own devices and brought each other up.

My mother and her siblings are classic examples of a dysfunctional upbringing. As adults, the four women chose their men badly and suffered affairs, violence, emotional abuse and loneliness. Although the men chose their partners well, they both had their fair share of issues. All six had two or three children each, and the last time I saw any of my cousins it was clear that we were all (in some way or other) still reeling from what we had gone through. None of us were spared our parents' dysfunctions.

My mother was deeply affected by her childhood and she emerged from it knowing that she wanted a better start for her own children. There was no way she would go out to work all hours leaving her family behind once she was a mum. She wanted a family desperately and felt that constantly being present would be enough to ensure her kids grew up happy. Unfortunately, the reality couldn't have been further from what she intended.

Rather than dealing with the past, healing herself and gaining some life experience, she rushed into having a baby with my biological father when she was 18. A man who abandoned her to marry the woman he was engaged to throughout their brief affair. She then did the exact same thing less than two years later with my stepfather; she'd only known him for a few months before falling pregnant with my half-brother. My half-sister came along three years later even though they were not a proper couple.

From my earliest memories it was apparent that my family was not normal, but I always knew my path was straightforward. I would not just talk about how my kids would have a better childhood than the one I had yet still rush into having babies anyway. I would do everything in my power to become emotionally stable before bringing children into the world, and once they were here I would ensure that I did not repeat history. In my early twenties I honestly didn't think I had a maternal instinct. I was far too busy with experiencing as much of what life had to offer to be getting broody.

For me, breaking the cycle meant finding true happiness within myself. I then had to settle down with a suitable partner before even entertaining the idea of starting a family. I found my husband long before I found inner peace, but both were firmly in place before falling pregnant with our eldest daughter.

Now that I'm a mum I know with absolute certainty that I would not have coped well with the trials and tribulations of motherhood had I not fully dealt with my demons and put the past to rest before having my children. I also know that I wouldn't be half the person I am today without the support of my wonderful husband

and amazing friends. This is a chicken and egg situation, because without becoming the best me I would not have kept hold of the fantastic people I have in my life.

I believe that most negative behaviour patterns lead back to a cycle of dysfunction, and you can apply the rule to almost any negative situation. The hardest part can be realising the cycle exists in the first place. I feel that once you are able to recognise the cycle and are committed to breaking it, you're halfway there. You have to be willing to unlearn things that have been passed down from your family, and shun deeply-ingrained thought processes. It's time to start truly thinking for yourself.

If you have a cycle to break yet do nothing to actively break it, you will almost certainly pass your dysfunctions on to your children one day. The cycle has to stop with you to ensure they are given the very best start to life that you can possibly offer them. If you are already a parent then please do not feel the opportunity has been lost. As long as you are 100% committed to the cause, the cycle can be broken at any time. Today is a good day to start your journey.

More examples of the cycle of dysfunction

Emotional and physical abuse

- Growing up in a violent environment, then going on to become violent yourself or having a partner that is violent towards you.

- Growing up watching one parent always putting the other one down, destroying their self-confidence with every comment. You may do the same as an adult or have a partner who is derogatory towards you but feel you do not deserve any better.

- Watching a parent be cheated on and generally treated badly by the other, then going on to treat your own partners badly or being treated badly yourself.

Health issues

- Growing up around alcoholics or drug addicts and developing addictions yourself. It's imperative that you wake up to these addictions and seek help as soon as possible.

- Having a bad diet as a child which has led to weight and/or psychological problems as a result. If you were never taught how to cook and are still eating badly you are likely to be struggling with these issues well into adulthood.

- Some minor health complaints can be completely fixed and avoidable in the future through eating well and looking after our bodies.

Other examples

- You may have felt you were a disappointment to your parents when you were growing up which has led to having low self-esteem. If your parents expected too much from you as a child, this could lead to feeling that nothing you ever do is enough.

- Not being good with money and getting into debt while you are young is a curse. If your parents were bad with their cash then you have never known any other way of life.

What separates the cycle breakers from the cycle repeaters?

The million pound question seems to be: What is the fundamental difference between a person capable of breaking the cycle, and a person who goes on to repeat history and continue it? The answer is of course complex, with too many variables to pinpoint any one defining factor. I believe that there are three core steps we need to go through to break the cycle. We will look at each of them in depth throughout the book.

Step One: Awareness

It can seem so much easier to just ignore our problems in the hope that they disappear, but they never do. In fact they become harder to deal with as time goes on. To break the cycle you have to acknowledge that it exists in the first place. Self-reflection can be a bitter pill to swallow but it is absolutely necessary during this process. There will be lots of looking long and hard at yourself, and the company you keep, to assess the changes that need to be made so you get to become the best you. No matter how bad your earlier life has been or how messed up you think you are, it is down to you and you alone to secure your future happiness. No-one else can do this for you.

Step Two: Determination

Breaking the cycle is hard work, and some people think they simply do not possess the tenacity to do the job. It is much easier to just follow in the footsteps of our parents because it's all we have ever known, but if you want to have a different life you will need to do things differently. Waking up to wanting more is a massive step in the right direction, but you'll have to surround yourself with the very best people in order for it to happen. A supportive partner, real friends or loving family will want to help you, not try to sabotage your efforts. People who genuinely love you would only ever want to encourage your success. You have to be strong and not let anyone take advantage of you. If certain people are bringing you down then you'll need to be prepared to get some distance from them.

Step Three: Courage

You will have to get to know yourself, and always be true to who you really are. This means not getting swept up with the crowd, and never living your life according to anyone else's timetable. You will need to be a 'what you see is what you get' type of person, not someone who changes their personality based on who they happen to be with at that moment. Anyone can put on a brave face but a cycle breaker will have a truly positive attitude towards life. Once we are thinking positively we start acting positively and after a short while it becomes our natural default setting. Cycle breakers do not sit around waiting for a lottery win or dream job to fall at their feet, they make stuff happen. Ultimately it's one thing talking about change, but actually changing is a huge challenge. You must always have the courage of your own convictions, stay focused and believe without doubt that you are doing the right thing.

Chapter Two

A Little about Me

"Be who you are and say what you feel. Those who mind don't matter, and those who matter don't mind." *Dr. Seuss*

I WAS mostly 'dragged up'. After her own unhappy childhood, my mother had a baby (me) aged 18 because she wanted someone to love her. By the time she was 25, she had three kids. I had a different father to my siblings but she felt it was best to tell me their dad was also mine – the official lie being that he was in prison when I was born, explaining why he wasn't on my birth certificate. Growing up, it was obvious that he didn't love me as much as he did the other two, but I wasn't told the truth until after I had left home. It turns out my biological father was engaged to his current wife when he got my mother pregnant. To this day his wife does not know that I exist.

My stepfather had a horrendous childhood. His mother died when he was two, and he was shown very little love when he was younger. It's not surprising that he was a cold man. That he turned to crime. That he was an alcoholic, manic depressive and emotional bully. I remember being at my grandma's house one day when I was seven or eight years old, and having to go out to daddy's car and say goodbye because he was going to kill himself. He had a massive gun in the passenger seat and had drank so much he was paralytic. Although he didn't go through with it, that day haunted me for years.

He and my mother had a strange relationship. They only lived together as a couple for five years from when I was eleven, and split for good after that. I viewed him as a man of mystery throughout my entire childhood. We were not allowed to meet his family and I found out some years later it was because he'd had an affair with his sister-in-law and was the father of his brother's son. Apparently this boy and my half-brother were close in age and looked so similar they could have been twins. He knew the secret would have destroyed his brother so he sacrificed us instead.

He was overly generous when it came to birthdays and at Christmas time, which upset my mother as she felt he was flashing his cash as a slight towards her. Day to day he provided extras which went some way towards supplementing our benefits income, but she was terrible with the little money she had. I witnessed her many times putting her last pound into a fruit machine, or going to bingo with it. She was always hoping for a big win that would change our lives. In reality, the phone and electricity were cut off more times than I care to remember, and the cupboards were often bare. It was a constant battle to make ends meet and I grew up thinking that her life must have been utterly miserable.

Being the eldest, I was regularly left alone to babysit my half siblings from a very young age. One distinct memory shines through the rest. The remains of a Guy Fawkes bonfire rekindled and the garden caught light one evening while she was out. I was nine years old and seeing fire through the living room doors was absolutely terrifying. Fortunately our neighbours across the road were home and came to our rescue. Shortly after this my mother took in a friend's 16 year old son and he lived with us for a while. He would take advantage of me when she wasn't home which led to me having an unhealthy attitude towards men for many years afterwards.

My mother used to run up as much debt as she could get away with, and when it looked like it was catching up with her we would move house. Unbelievably, in the 1980s the debt would mainly be attached to your house rather than your name. By the early 1990s it was becoming harder to get away with, but not impossible. If there was a scam to be had she would seek it out. We'd had over a dozen addresses by the time I left home, which meant going to eight different schools.

I often endured low-level bullying for being the new girl and over the years I was spat at, sworn at, threatened with violence and routinely humiliated. The bullying I suffered in the last school I went to was significant, and led to a suicide attempt. I had gone to a sleepover and one of the boys molested me in my sleep. He then went into school and bragged about it. The police got involved and my so-called friends turned against me, saying it was all my fault. I found myself in the unfortunate position of being the most hated girl in the whole school. By then it was my final year and my self-esteem and confidence were at an all-time low. I loathed going in and would do anything for a day off, which meant falling behind with my work.

My stepfather was a permanent feature in our lives by then, and the best way to describe him was that he was a deeply unhappy, 'functioning' alcoholic. We got into a fight one morning about me not wanting to go to school and he punched me in the face. He was often harsh with his words but usually kept his fists to himself. He almost broke my nose, and this ended up being the catalyst for me leaving home. I was 15, had no qualifications and only £50 in my pocket. He said I'd be pregnant and living in a hovel within the year. I went to stay with an aunt in her tiny maisonette where I slept on the floor of my cousin's bedroom between the cot and the bunk beds. It wasn't ideal but at least I was safe.

No-one escapes the psychological fallout of a childhood like mine. I went through major bouts of depression as a young adult, and lived life in self-destruct mode for many years to numb my pain. I spent my teens and early twenties going from one all-weekend bender to the next. I had a string of disastrous relationships early on, then spent a handful of years sleeping with just about anyone. I wouldn't have even looked at half of them once, let alone twice, when I was sober.

Eventually I had a breakdown aged 22 and sought professional help. My counsellor was an amazing women who had lots of experience dealing with family dramas. During the eighteen months that I saw her regularly she taught me that I needed distance from my family, that I deserved to be loved and how to respect myself. Although she tried her hardest she couldn't get me to tackle my love of booze or partying. That would come later. Along with breakdown number two.

Even though my finger was firmly attached to the self-destruct button, I knew from day one that it was up to me to fend for myself and have always worked. My first few jobs were cash in hand affairs in grimy market caffs and pound shops. As soon as I had my National Insurance number I went searching for something that paid more money and offered more respect. After working in retail for a year or so a friend suggested I learn some computer skills and try finding an office job.

It was great advice. I worked locally to gain some basic experience, but being the only non-family member in a small office I was treated like a second class citizen. It wasn't exactly the step up I was hoping for, and as soon as I felt competent enough around the computer I set my sights higher.

One sunny day, armed only with a flimsy CV and the ability to talk the hind legs off a donkey, I ventured into the City of London and went door knocking on recruitment agencies. After a lot of rejection someone offered me a temp job on the reception desk of a major financial corporation. I knew it was a huge opportunity, and I worked my socks off to ensure that they would keep me on after my initial two weeks. I was given an administration role and stayed for three years, after which I moved to a company around the corner for a decent pay bump.

When I was made redundant after two and a half years I was given a £10,000 pay-out. It was the most money I'd ever had and I decided to book myself an around the world ticket and go travelling. I had so much fun and met lots of interesting people; a good handful of them are still a part of my life. The trip was the best decision I ever made because it was where I met the man I now call my husband. I'd been on the road for almost six months at that point and in South East Asia for two.

Andy and I met on Serendipity Beach in Cambodia. It was supposed to be my last night in the town before heading to Laos, and it was his first night there. I had been out to dinner with some friends and we went to our favourite bar afterwards for a nightcap. I spotted him as soon as I walked in and introduced myself right away. Sparks flew and if this doesn't qualify as 'love at first sight' then I have no idea what does. We stayed up talking all night and the next morning had breakfast together and chatted away for over four hours. We clearly had a connection. Not only was he handsome and my type but he was down to earth and easy company. He was just what I needed and I decided to get an extension on my Cambodian visa and travel the country some more with him.

We spent six blissful weeks together and each day was an adventure. When we went our separate ways (him to Australia and me home) it was awful, we missed each other so much. After just three days in the UK I realised I was making a huge mistake, and within a fortnight I was on a flight heading to Melbourne. My future was uncertain and funds were fast running out but I knew I would regret not going and seeing what could have been. We spent our first six months together living and working in Australia, then went back to Asia for a little holiday before returning to the UK. Neither of us could properly settle at home though because Cambodia had gotten well and truly under our skin.

We headed back out there longer-term around our first anniversary. The original plan was to find English teaching jobs, but we were given the opportunity to set up a shop above an established charity. By day we sold clothes and other tourist trinkets then four nights a week we became the Revelation Vodka Bar, specialising in different flavoured vodkas that I had created. The paint had barely dried when a spiral of events caused me to reach boiling point with my mother, and I made the tough decision to cut ties with her. I will tell you more about this in the chapter entitled: "Call Time on Toxic Relationships".

Although I now view it as one of the best decisions I have ever made, at the time it sent me to a very dark place. I pushed Andy away, crossed the line to the wrong side of partying and was completely out of control. I was hardly eating and existed mainly on iced coffee during the day, then I'd drink vodka all evening and well into the early hours. I wasn't averse to hanging out in undesirable places either, getting wasted with the wasters. I had a sizeable Valium addiction by this stage, and would regularly take other powerful pharmaceutical drugs. My sense of what was normal and acceptable became more and more skewed each and every day. I honestly feel that had we stayed in Cambodia any longer I would have ended up dead.

When we returned home almost a year to the day after we left, it was separately. We then had an on/off relationship for months which must have driven our friends crazy. During this time I worked for a small company with high expectations of me, both professionally and socially. I used to work 12-hour days, then go out drinking until the early morning at least three times a week. After living like this for about six months I ended things with Andy 'for good this time'. A few weeks after we split I went on the quarterly work social weekend. An all-expenses paid trip to Reykjavik. After parting non-stop for 36 hours and being so wasted I picked a fight with my boss, I took a taxi alone from the bar to my hotel on the other side of town.

When I woke up the next morning I was utterly appalled with myself. I had gone too far this time. I'd argued with my boss, shown myself up in front of my colleagues and put myself in unnecessary danger once again. I looked in the mirror and told myself that enough was enough. This nonsense had to stop right here and right now. It was my 'rock bottom'. The penny had finally dropped. This is when I woke up to myself and my addictions and decided to get clean. Rock bottom came with the epiphany that I was in great danger of losing the best thing that had ever happened to me. The gravity of my foolishness hit me like a whack in the face, and for the first time in a very long time I did something right.

I worked incredibly hard to become a better person than the one I was perhaps 'destined' to be, given my background and start in life. I didn't so much as sniff an alcoholic drink for three months, then I learnt self-control, something that had been absent until that point. I disassociated myself from bad influences and stopped partying. I knuckled down at work. I read lots of self-help books and developed a truly positive mental attitude. Above all else, I became happy with what I saw in the mirror and started enjoying my own company.

After three months of no contact I got in touch with my then ex and told him about the new me. Fortunately he gave me one last chance, and we headed into a fresh year under very different circumstances. I was no longer unable to have a glass of wine without finishing the bottle. I didn't want to go out partying all night anymore. Fast forward to today and I am a happily married mum of three. I'm highly regarded among my peers and considered to be well-rounded and dependable: a good mother, wife and friend.

There are people who you meet who seem to easily breeze through life. It's as if they were born under a lucky star and it follows them everywhere. On the flip side, other poor souls get the rawest end of the bargain. For most of us though, how we deal with the hand we are dealt determines our fortune. The way I see it is this: we all have control over our own destiny. It is up to each of us to ensure that we live our lives being the best we can possibly be.

I truly believe that anyone can change their ways, no matter how naughty or wicked. Anyone is capable of breaking the cycle of dysfunction as I did. You just have to want to badly enough.

Chapter Three

RESPECT YOURSELF

"Respect your efforts, respect yourself. Self-respect leads to self-discipline. When you have both firmly under your belt, that's real power." *Clint Eastwood*

GIVEN THAT you're reading this book you are likely to have had troubles in your life. Perhaps you were abused as a child. Or bullied at school or in the workplace. Perhaps you witnessed your parents go through a horrible messy divorce when you were a kid. Perhaps you've had bad relationships that have left your confidence in tatters. Or maybe you just lost your way and have turned to booze, drugs or food for comfort and escapism. Whatever your reasons are, they will almost always lead back to a dysfunctional past.

The only way to move on and properly heal is by being brutally honest with yourself. Admitting that you are troubled and pinpointing the cause is the first step towards breaking the cycle. Getting to the very root of our problems, even though it will involve dredging up painful memories, is the best way to ensure they are properly dealt with. Sweeping them under the carpet and pretending they don't exist isn't an option, it will only lead to long-term heartache. Unless you make peace with your past and forgive the wrongdoings of yesterday, and all parties involved, you will always be glancing backwards and won't be able to focus on ensuring that tomorrow is a better day.

Forgiving ourselves and those who have caused us pain

When we have been through trauma and stress, especially if it involves abuse, our confidence often takes the brunt and can all but disappear. Other people's words or actions can be tremendously damaging for many years after the event. However, if you are to break the cycle you must not let your life be defined by tragic and unhappy past events. You cannot allow yourself to be a victim. Take back control from those who have taken it from you.

It's important now to stop torturing yourself over the things you have done before because absolutely no good will come of you beating yourself up. Put in the simplest terms the past cannot be changed so it's best to accept it for what it was and move forwards with life. It is just as essential to let go of the hurt caused by those who have brought you pain. What has happened has already been done and cannot be taken back. Acceptance is the only solution. Rather than dwelling over what has gone on before, truly learn from the mistakes that have been made by not making them again. Repeating the same negative behaviour will only lead to the same negative outcome.

If you know you have caused someone else pain and you feel bad about it, reach out to them and apologise. Call them; send them a gift or a card; say the words 'I'm sorry' and sincerely mean it. A genuine apology will go a long way to help rebuild damaged relationships. Apologising and trying to make amends will also help to ease your guilty conscience. If the other person will allow you to, you can prove that you want to start afresh. If they're not interested then at least you will know you've done the right thing and given it your best shot. As long as we put the experience to good use in the future there can be many valuable lessons to be learnt from failed relationships. All does not have to be lost.

It doesn't have to be complicated but I would like to suggest you devise a set of basic principles to live by. Say them in front of the mirror each morning like a mantra. Embrace them fully and believe in them until they are deeply ingrained. When you're having a tough day, repeat them in your head over and again. Here are a few examples:

'I will be true to myself today.'

'I will be kind to myself and those around me today.'

'I will make good decisions today.'

Make better decisions

Most of us have done things in our lives that we aren't
very proud of, but admitting the error of our ways is
a brave thing to do. Changing for the better has to
start with making good decisions. If you grew up in
an environment where the adults were setting bad
examples and you weren't taught right from wrong,
then you will need to learn it. Let's fine-tune your moral
compass and work on your life choices.

During this process you won't need to hide away and
become boring, but you may need to remove yourself
from certain situations to stop doing things that make
you feel bad about yourself. This will mean taking the
time to properly think over your decisions to ensure you
are making the best ones possible. We want decisions
that will lead to happy events, not further upset. Avoid
doing things that give anyone else the opportunity
to hold leverage over you, or throw those things back
in your face at a later date. Occupy your time in a
productive way; don't waste it on people who don't
deserve you or situations that will damage you.

By not putting ourselves into precarious situations in the first place nothing bad can happen as a result. Often we do things because they are easy or because they have become a habit, but all habits can be broken if we put our minds to it. If you know that socialising with certain people always leads to trouble, the next time you are invited out with them politely decline. Try it as soon as you can; I bet it's easier than you think it will be. Instead, treat yourself to a night at home with your favourite movie and truly relish the peace.

When we are surrounded by bad influences it can be very difficult to think clearly. They can cloud our judgement which leads to us doing things that we don't really want to do. This in turn makes us unhappy, and leads to low self-esteem. We have to turn this around and get you liking yourself. It's time to decide who has a place in your life; let's start thinking about how your friends and family make you feel. Is anyone taking advantage of you? Do you give too much and feel that your relationships are one-sided? Are certain people causing you to be miserable more often than not? We will discuss this more throughout the book.

Confidence is key

Having confidence in our own abilities is so much more than an external front. Once you start respecting yourself and have stopped doing things that make you miserable, over time your confidence levels should start to grow. I believe that confidence is vital if we are to drag ourselves out of a rut and move forward with our lives. When we conduct ourselves with integrity and carry ourselves with genuine confidence, it inspires faith in those around us. It will shine through every word that comes out of your mouth. There are many ways to give ourselves a boost, here are a few examples:

- Walk tall and smile! Hold your head up high and face the world with a massive grin on your face. These two tiny changes can be implemented immediately and have a dramatic effect.

- Do something that takes you out of your comfort zone and scares you a little. This can be anything from participating in a class or course to skydiving out of an aeroplane. It could be throwing a dinner party and cooking the food from scratch for the very first time all by yourself. Whatever you decide, I'm sure you will be impressed with your own capabilities.

- Start a hobby and become really good at it. The only way we master skills is by practising them over and over again. If you've always fancied turning your hand to something new but haven't managed to before, now is the time.

When your self-respect and confidence are firmly in place you can start living, breathing (and most importantly) believing in the power of YOU each and every day! There is absolutely no point in sitting around talking about changing your life if you don't actually think that you are capable of pulling it off. Anything is possible but you have to be willing to work hard to make it happen.

A suggested plan of action

Visualise: Start visualising the person you want to be and the things you would like to achieve in life. Read up on the people you most admire and how they got to where they are today. A healthy dose of inspiration can work wonders for our own motivation and creativity.

Positivity: Look for the positives in every situation and focus on all that is going well in your world. If you're feeling low take a walk through your local park, stopping every now and then to appreciate the beautiful trees. No matter how dire our situation there is always something good to be found in nature.

Confidence: Do something small every day to boost your confidence and make you feel good about yourself. From taking extra pride in your appearance to learning a new skill, there are opportunities to give yourself a boost to be found everywhere.

Above all else at this early stage of the process: Make peace with your past no matter how dark or painful it is. Otherwise it will haunt you forever!

Chapter Four

TAKE RESPONSIBILITY

"No one can make you feel inferior without your consent." *Eleanor Roosevelt*

IN THE first few years after I left home, I got myself into all kinds of undesirable situations. Sometimes through naively trusting people, often through being intoxicated and making terrible decisions. Here are a few examples:

- Leaving myself jobless and homeless on the promise of money to go travelling (from my mother) that didn't materialise. It all turned out to be a ploy to get me to come back to where she was living.

- Sleeping with a friend's very recent ex-boyfriend (while drunk) and losing her and her two sisters' friendship. They were also flatmates so this prompted a house move.

- Putting myself into unnecessary danger countless times by going back to random strangers' houses after clubbing. I recall scanning the room on more occasions than I care to remember and realising that I was the only female. Panicked thoughts would run through my head: *Where am I? No-one knows I'm here! What if this turns nasty? Six blokes and me, I wouldn't stand a chance!* I count myself really lucky than nothing too awful ever happened as a result.

There are many more scrapes I got myself into, but this chapter would be too long if I included them all. I had to learn my lessons the hard way, through the harsh reality of living them and facing the consequences of my actions. It wasn't always pretty, in fact at points it was out-and-out ugly, but I can honestly say now that I'm grateful for the colourful life I've had. At the age of 35 I feel that all those bad experiences have made me the person I am today, and if I had my time over I doubt I would change a single thing.

I am also aware that looking at the past through rose-coloured glasses with the benefit of hindsight is a wonderful thing. Unsurprisingly at the time I didn't feel too overjoyed by the crappy stuff that was happening. I have had several periods of my life where just getting out of bed in the morning was an effort.

Getting help

When I had my first breakdown at 22 I knew the time had come to seek professional help, and I look at this as a very significant part of my history. I strongly believe that the counselling I went through back then plays a huge role in my ability to function and live a normal life now. I know with absolute certainty that I am only capable of being the wife and mum I am today because I made peace with my past way before I started thinking about having a family of my own.

My counsellor, Nina, came highly recommended to me by a person I trusted, at a time in my life when I desperately needed guidance. I was fortunate that she and I instantly clicked. Nina was very patient and understanding and when she offered up her nuggets of wisdom it was never in a way that I felt patronised by. I always wanted to take her advice on board and put it into action so I could tell her about it the next time I saw her.

Nina opened my eyes to how much of a drain on my emotional resources my family were. That they were forever taking from me in some way or another, yet rarely giving me anything in return. That this wasn't normal and I shouldn't just be putting up with it because they were related to me. She helped change the way I viewed myself and made me realise that I deserved more out of life than I was getting. Most of all, Nina taught me

43

that I needed to love myself, because if I didn't then how could I expect anyone else to?

You cannot put a price on your mental health, it's a vitally important part of your wellbeing. If you are unhappy then your world simply will not work properly. After a dysfunctional childhood or early experience one of the worst things to have to admit to yourself is that you are all alone in the world, but it's time to face up to this and stop blaming others for how your life is going. Your happiness is in your own hands and no-one else's. Regardless of what you have been through before now, and whose fault it was, it is up to you to take back control and make your future a brighter place.

There are lots of ways you can seek help to support you through troubled times. If you feel you need professional help then it's essential you get it in whatever form you are comfortable with. Although counselling got me back on track, and I cannot advocate it enough, I'm aware that it's not for everyone.

Other ways you can seek help

Intervention: Arrange a gathering and get the deep dark secrets that are causing pain out in the open. Talk them through with the people involved and agree to forgive and forget. If you are all willing to work together as a team it could be easier than you think to put those secrets into a box and bury them in a safe place where they can't hurt you anymore.

Group therapy: If you have specific problems you need to address, then joining a support group could be the answer you're looking for. Not only might it help you to overcome these problems, you could also make new like-minded friends, or find a mentor. Someone that has been exactly where you are right now could help you with implementing the changes you need to become the best you.

Life coaching: If you feel you are lacking direction and need some guidance, a good life coach will assist with getting you on to the right path. It's commonly misunderstood that life coaches and counsellors are one and the same, but this is not the case. If a life coach is doing their job properly they should be encouraging you to make the decisions you already know need to be made. They won't bring up the past the whole time, and you shouldn't need too many sessions.

Self-help books: Reading inspirational books can be a positive and uplifting experience, which you can have in the comfort of your own home without having to involve anyone else. If you think you might opt for counselling in the future but aren't quite ready for it yet, I would suggest reading far and wide on all subjects you feel you could benefit from. As a generic starting point I can personally recommend the following:

- *The Art of Happiness* by The Dalai Lama

- *They F*** You Up* by Oliver James

- *You Can Heal Your Life* by Louise Hay

Writing: Cathartic writing can be a fantastic way of getting old and unwanted memories out of your head. Even if it initially causes upset, over time you will probably get a lot out of it. They say everybody has a book in them; why not put the theory to the test and see if it's true?

Detox: Consider following a simple liver detox for a month. When we are drinking or partying or eating lots of junk it can be very difficult to look at situations objectively. A liver cleanse will help to clear your head and put you in a good position to start doing some life laundry. Always consult with your GP beforehand.

Meditation: Learning how to properly calm your body and mind will help to restore some peace in your chaotic world. Meditating is incredibly grounding and a really useful skill to have. Pick a quiet space and focus on your breathing. With your eyes and mouth closed take slow deep breaths in and out through your nose. Try to completely clear your mind and concentrate solely on your breathing. Begin with a few minutes at the very start of each day and slowly increase over time.

Identifying negative behaviour

When we're engrossed in the cycle of dysfunction we are often our own worst enemies, and although brutal self-reflection can be painful in the short term it is absolutely necessary if we are to successfully change our lives.
To break the cycle we need to be become self-aware. Hopefully, by now, you are ready to start identifying behaviour patterns that are detrimental to your life. Behaviour such as: drinking too much; addictions; sleeping around; over-eating for comfort; self-harming; and spending more than you earn. If you can identify with any of these examples then you will need to start doing things differently.

A few suggestions

Drinking: Having a couple of drinks to get into the swing of a party is fine, but if you always take drinking to the extreme and it leads to trouble, then you must stop pushing the boundaries quite so far. If you don't feel you have the will power to hold back then don't go out in the first place. It took me three months of complete abstinence from booze then another three months to learn the self-control I desperately needed. Your length of abstinence might be shorter or longer than mine depending on your situation, but some time off the sauce will definitely be required. It's important to remember that change will not happen overnight, so be patient with yourself during this time.

Money: Spending more money than you earn could lead to massive debts and eventual bankruptcy. Think about subtle lifestyle changes you could make to save cash. Could your car be downgraded? Do you need state of the art technology? Could you buy less expensive clothes? Do you go out to bars and restaurants that you can't afford? Start weighing up your wants against your needs and think about whether you really need the things you are spending your money on.

Sex: Harmless fun can be great between two single and fully consenting adults. If, however, you regularly find yourself in bed with people that you aren't even attracted to, then you probably experience a fair amount of self-loathing as a result. If you are not truly comfortable with casual sex and would prefer to have meaningful relationships then you'll have to stop sleeping around. I would also strongly recommend that you never share naked photos of yourself with anyone. You don't know where they could end up.

Identifying bad influences

Now is also the time to identify the bad influences in your life because you will never break the cycle if you spend your time with people who are dragging you down. It's important to remember that all relationships need to be nurtured by both parties and it should never feel like you are doing all the giving or all the taking. If this is the case then things must change for it to become fairer. Takers will sap your energy and leave you feeling drained and unhappy; don't let them take from you for a moment longer. Take back control!

There's a theory that we will only ever be as good as the five people we spend the most time with. Ask yourself these tough questions, and start thinking of the answers: Do the people in your life enhance it, or do some of them make it more difficult? Will they be able to achieve all the things you want to achieve? Are you heading in different directions, and if so do you have a long-term future? We will look at this in depth later in the book.

A suggested plan of action

Gremlins: Start viewing your negative behavioural tendencies as little gremlins that make you do things you don't really want to do. Take control back from them and squash those little monsters by practising self-control as much as you possibly can.

49

Honesty: Be completely honest at all times by self-reflecting. Truly learn as many lessons as you can from your mistakes and put what you've learnt to good use by not repeating them.

Selfless: Consider doing more for other people. Volunteer for your local charity shop; help an elderly neighbour or take a meal to a person who has just had a baby. Selfless acts will take your mind off your own troubles and help you to feel good about yourself. They will also make the other person's day.

Chapter Five

FIND YOUR INNER STRENGTH

"You never know how strong you are, until being strong is your only choice." *Bob Marley*

ALTHOUGH WRITING a rigid life plan could potentially backfire and set you up for disaster, having an idea of which direction you want to head can only be a good thing. If you are aiming for fortune and/or fame, then it's wise to have a back-up. Being talent-spotted in the street or winning £100 million on the lottery carry the same kind of odds, and are almost definitely not going to happen to you or anyone you know. It's time for a realistically optimistic outlook, and to see what you are capable of achieving. Stop getting bogged down with the problems and instead start figuring out the solutions!

Have you fallen into the trap of thinking that money will solve everything? I can safely say that although money can make life more comfortable, money alone will never guarantee happiness. It is absolutely imperative to become a happy person first and is utterly pointless pinning all your hopes on an elusive windfall. Even if millions did land at your feet they would mean nothing if you were not happy beforehand. Once you like yourself, are surrounded by good people, and are content with your life, you will be rich in your own right. In this chapter we will talk about all the things I have done over the years to boost my own happiness; I hope they work as well for you.

A sunny outlook on life

A positive mental attitude is essential if you are to break the cycle, and although it doesn't come naturally to a lot of people it will get you far. There is absolutely no point in putting on a brave face and adopting an air of positivity unless you genuinely believe in it, though. Positive thinking is addictive and infectious and once you are emanating happiness others around you should soon follow suit. Over time I'm sure you will find yourself really enjoying the new positive you and won't have to work so hard at it any more.

I used to think that people who were always happy must be faking it and putting it on for the benefit of others, but now I realise otherwise. I was the one who wasn't capable of true happiness back then because my life was in such a mess. I was the one who wasn't able to be happy every day and I assumed everyone else was the same. But we're not. When we *assume*, we make an ASS of U and ME, so it's always best to try and gather the facts instead. By not assuming you might be pleasantly surprised to find that some situations aren't as bad as you thought they were.

Social networks

In the world of social networks people rarely post photos of themselves looking like they need to go on a diet or buy acne cream. For the most part they are trying to create the illusion that all is fabulous and they have the trappings of a 'perfect life'. Even though in our heart of hearts we know that it's all being put on for show, it is so easy to end up thinking that everyone else is faring better than we are. Ask yourself how much of your time goes on social networking sites and how they make you feel as a result. If you feel they are a lifeline and provide you with nothing but happiness then great, you don't need to change anything. If you end up comparing yourself to others and it causes you sadness then we need to think of a solution.

Completely coming off any social network can feel like a big statement which most of us are not prepared to make, but scaling down the amount of time we spend on these sites can be really beneficial. I used to feel the need to check my news feeds hourly but I can now easily go an entire day without looking at all. I got bored of the same people posting the same things; the silent stalkers; alpha mums and pushy parents. For me it was another habit that needed to be broken. I feel social networks have their place, but they are also a time-suck and I know I'm better off without the constant distraction. Although at first it was strange, and sometimes people would assume I knew things because they had posted them publicly, I got used to the new situation pretty quickly. I have come to the conclusion that genuine friends will want to share their lives with me in real life, and they won't hold it against me if I don't comment on every single status update.

A simple strategy for cutting down

Make it less easy: Delete the apps from your phone or tablet as it can be too tempting to click on them every time you have a spare five minutes. By having to log into an actual computer you are making it more difficult to be permanently 'plugged in'.

Cold turkey: See if you can last an entire day without logging in at all. I promise you the world will not stop turning, and you might find that it's a surprisingly liberating experience. You could post a status the day before with your plans and challenge your friends to do the same. It could be fun to see who is willing to join you, and who was able to last the day.

Little by little: When you feel ready to cut down begin with logging in three times a day, then after a week cut down to twice a day and after another week cut down to once. By gradually reducing the time you spend on these sites you should still feel part of the loop, and not that you are missing out on anything important.

Consume your information wisely

While you are going through this process I'd like to highly recommend not watching what I call 'scheduled junk' (aka Reality TV). Would it be the end of the world if you didn't know who got to the final of the latest so-called talent contest? Does it really matter if a new series of people sitting around a house all day has just started? Or that a handful of Z list celebrities are eating spiders in the jungle? What do you really get out of these shows? What's in it for you?

Rather than letting others dictate how you should be entertaining yourself, take back control by making quality viewing choices. Don't just watch what everyone else is watching because you're worried that you might be left out of the conversation. These shows are addictive because they are intrinsically linked to the advertising industry. Advertising is big business and millions are pumped into the industry every single day to make their job as sleek as possible. They exist solely for one purpose and that is to sell you stuff! Adverts are full of portrayals of the 'perfect life' which can leave us feeling inferior and gloomy.

While you're at it ditch mainstream news, papers and magazines as well. They are full of shocking and depressing stories that can leave unwanted thoughts and images in our heads that can be detrimental to our happiness. If you want to keep yourself well-informed you could scan a reputable news website instead. I'm not saying for a second that you shouldn't know anything outside of your own life and live in a bubble, but I think being selective about the information we consume is a good idea. Rather than waste your time and money on trashy TV and magazines, start spending it wisely. Here are a few suggestions of what you could do instead:

- Read a book that you've been wanting to read for ages but haven't got round to. Reading books in their paper form can be a magical experience which is not replicated on electronic devices. Browse your local library or charity shop for free or low-cost options.

- Work your way through a boxed set or good film that you've been wanting to watch but haven't had the time to. Catch up channels and streaming websites are full to the brim with fantastic telly, and many of them do not have adverts.

- Use your spare time productively by learning valuable life skills. Be it cooking good food, taking better photographs or turning your hand to DIY, practise often and you will get better. You can then share your new-found skills with the people you love and respect.

Control your thoughts

While I was feeling my worst, negative thoughts and flashbacks to dark memories used to take over my mind. They would muddy almost everything else I tried to think about, leaving me anxiety-ridden and stuck in the past. During the recovery period after my second breakdown I realised that if I didn't learn to control my thoughts they would eventually end up controlling me.

It took a few months of diverting my mind elsewhere every single time I had these thoughts, but I trained myself to switch my brain off and think of other things instead. It was a huge problem for me, so I made it my mission to change it, and I can honestly say that I can't remember the last time I felt it was an issue. The simple distraction techniques detailed below worked really well for me. Try one of them next time you need to banish unwanted thoughts from your head.

- Close your eyes, concentrate on your breathing and picture yourself on a memorable holiday or during a fantastic experience. Transport yourself there and remember how happy you were in that moment. From now on this becomes your 'happy place' and it is always accessible, ready to pick you up whenever you're feeling down.

- Recite something familiar in your head such as the lyrics to your favourite song, dialogue from a movie or a passage from a well-loved book. This works in the same way that counting sheep can help to fall asleep. Mundane tasks such as these will take your mind off the unwanted thoughts.

- Look into the mirror, smile and tell yourself that you will not think about those things. Instead you will think about the good stuff going on in your life. Divert your attention to happiness, plain and simple.

Work hard

No-one I know was ever given amazing opportunities unless they deserved them. Dream jobs do not fall into laps; it is up to us to make them happen. Rather than getting upset about not being recognised or rewarded enough, work harder and figure out how to set yourself apart from the crowd. Make yourself shine through with your confidence and capabilities. Take on extra projects and get yourself noticed by the people that make the decisions. Become an integral part of the team by making yourself as indispensable as you can.

Start thinking about what you really want to do with your life. If you're feeling unsatisfied at work then move role or company, don't resign yourself to a crappy career path just because it's easier to stay where you are. Look up careers advice online and seek some guidance from an expert. Think about the answers to the following questions; we will talk about this more in the next chapter.

- Can your current employer offer you another job in-house or would you need to leave the firm to progress?

- Would you need extra qualifications or training for a more desirable role? If so, could you gain them while working or would you need a break from the workplace? If so, could you cope financially?

- Is it worth thinking about moving abroad for the best opportunities?

Educate yourself by gaining knowledge on any subject matter that interests you. This is where the internet really comes into its own, because there will always be a blog, forum or website based around whatever it is that you want to learn about. If you are out of work then see what others are up to and get inspired. There are many incredible initiatives crying out for input from good people willing to work hard. Consider offering some assistance to a start-up or a charity for free to gain some valuable experience. Working for a company that excites you could ignite your own passions. It might also lead to paid employment eventually.

A suggested plan of action

Get happy: Think of your happy place as often as you can, especially as a way of banishing unwanted thoughts.

Switch off: Tune out from mass media by only consuming information that will enhance your life. Don't be dictated to by television companies, tabloids and trashy magazines.

Don't compare: There is a famous quote by Theodore Roosevelt that is worth remembering: 'Comparison is the thief of joy'. Stop comparing yourself to others because it's a pointless exercise. Instead, feel safe in the knowledge that no-one has the 'perfect life', we are all flawed in some way or another and everybody has problems. While you are lusting after another person's life, there will more than likely be someone out there lusting after yours. Forget about everyone else and concentrate on becoming the best possible you.

Chapter Six

FORM LIFELONG GOOD HABITS

"First we form habits, then they form us. Conquer your bad habits or they will conquer you." *Rob Gilbert*

ON THE surface big problems can seem overwhelmingly difficult to get past, but are much easier to tackle by being broken into small pieces and dealt with one at a time. When we make our problems smaller they become more manageable and easier to conquer. None of us are saints, and part of breaking the cycle means overcoming bad habits and facing our problems head on.

If you are to become the best you there will be certain things in your life that need to be done differently. In this chapter we will identify what those things are, and how you can successfully change them. In the same way that you'd write a list of New Year's resolutions, I'd like you to create a wishlist of all the things you would like to change about your life: everything from overcoming a classic 'bad habit' to wanting to find a new home or job. These will be your personal goals.

Devise a list of personal goals

To give you an example of how this would work in real life I have written what my own list of goals would have looked like when I was going through this process, along with all the things I had to do to achieve them. They are listed in three phases because although it wasn't clear to me at the time I now see that my goals were all linked.

My first goal was to cut down on drinking and it's obvious that without doing so I would not have been capable of achieving the rest of my goals. What I had to do and what I would advise you to do is pick the biggest, scariest one first because you will probably find the rest will naturally follow and things start falling into place after you have conquered it.

Phase One: The really important stuff

It will come as no surprise that top of my list was **CUTTING DOWN ON DRINKING**.

- After Reykjavik I realised I needed some time completely off alcohol, and when I first embarked on my period of abstinence I had no idea how long it would last. I wasn't sure if I'd pushed the boundaries so far that there would never be just a couple of social drinks ever again. I fully embraced abstinence, though, and it was exactly what I needed to start thinking clearly and making better decisions.

- Three months was enough of a break for me. After that I slowly reintroduced alcohol over the following three months by going out occasionally and having one or two drinks. It was during this time that I properly the learnt the self-control I desperately needed.

- It was tough but over time I got out of the mind-set that I was drinking to get drunk, and began enjoying good quality red wine or a well-made gin and tonic.

Next on my list was to **STOP SPENDING TIME WITH PEOPLE WHO ADDED NO VALUE TO MY LIFE** (drinking and clubbing buddies):

- Once I stopped drinking I realised how much of my time was spent socialising with people who did not enhance my life, so I simply excluded them from it. They were surprisingly easy to cut out and didn't fight very hard for my friendship.

- I told them I wasn't interested in partying anymore and they stopped inviting me out.

- I used to feel immense pressure to be sociable at work, but even this was easier to cut out than I thought it would be. After I made it clear I was off the sauce my colleagues soon lost interest in me. I thought this would upset me, and I'd feel left out, but it was a welcome relief.

Next up was to **STOP TAKING DRUGS**:

- This naturally followed the two points above. Once I had removed bad influences from my life and stopped drinking, I had no interest at all in going out clubbing. This meant not taking drugs anymore.

- Instead I spent lots of time at home. I read books, watched great TV, reconnected with good friends and most importantly became happy with my own company.

- The first few months were really hard because I knew that I'd hurt people and in the cold sober light of day I felt embarrassed and ashamed of my behaviour. This was an essential part of the process, though, because it allowed me the time and perspective I needed to figure out who was worth keeping in my life.

Phase Two: Essential, but only achievable after conquering the really important stuff first

Top of this list was to **START EATING BETTER:**

- I had fallen into the trap of buying most things pre-prepared due to lack of time, so I went back to basics. I started ordering my groceries online, planning what I was going to eat for the week and cooking everything from scratch again. Not going out drinking and clubbing meant that I had loads more time on my hands for the important things in my life.

- I also started taking my own food into work which as well as being healthier saved money.

- I quickly had more energy and didn't feel tired all the time.

Next up was to **START EXERCISING AGAIN:**

- I found some suitable DVDs and set aside a few timeslots per week to establish a home work-out routine.

- It quickly became a part of my weekly schedule and I fell in love with exercising, whereas I had previously seen it as a chore, something I should be doing but didn't particularly enjoy.

- It gave me a great confidence boost when I most needed it.

Next up was to **STOP WASTING MONEY** on unnecessary things:

- I naturally saved a fortune when I stopped going out partying.

- I started shopping for clothes and other essential items in charity shops or heavily reduced sales. I became mindful of weighing up my wants against my true needs and realised that I didn't need a lot of the stuff I thought I did.

- I still buy clothes secondhand nowadays. Not only does it save money but it's friendlier to the environment.

Phase Three: Very important goal lurking in the background, only achievable after months of research and getting to grips with the rest of my goals first

I only had one thing on this list, and it was to **FIND A NEW JOB:**

- I stayed in the same job for seven months after the Reykjavik incident. Not because I wanted to but because I was not capable of doing something new until I had conquered the first two phases of my list.

- During this time I did a lot of thinking and realised what I wanted more than anything else career-wise was to work for myself, so I set up a small food business. Looking back I rushed into it, and I paid the price by being left bankrupt and having to liquidate the company within its first year. I view this as a positive experience overall, though. It taught me some very valuable life lessons, especially where money is concerned.

- I went back to admin afterwards and have been working part-time since having children. I currently work two days a week in a job that I enjoy for a company that values me. I still aspire to work for myself again someday, but next time I'll ensure I have a watertight business plan.

Become dedicated to the cause

Making my changes and establishing good routines took me about six months, during which I learnt that patience really is a virtue. My list was quite a tall order and trying to do it all at once would have been be near-on impossible. I focused my energies on one goal at a time and I'd suggest you do the same. By working on them this way you are more likely to succeed.

To stay on track, ensure that you continually recognise your efforts and reward yourself justly. Begin by setting yourself daily targets, and progress to weekly targets once you are comfortable with what you need to do. Think of a nice little treat for yourself when you meet or exceed your target, as you'll be one step closer to achieving your goals. By doing this you are holding yourself to account as well as recognising your hard work. This is another way to make yourself feel good and will provide a confidence boost. Here are a few tips for staying on track:

- Ensure that your targets are high enough to count but low enough to attain as it will help keep you motivated. If your targets are too high, or you try to do too much at once, you could be setting yourself up for failure. This in turn could lead to losing interest in your goals altogether. Don't trip over the first hurdle and fall for this common mistake.

- Whether you are in the market for a new job, home or hobby, ensure that you do your research and find out as much relevant background information as you can beforehand. You can never be too prepared for a job interview, so do your best to woo your potential future employer with your knowledge on the company and role. These small details make all the difference at the hiring stage.

- Rejection is tough but you must not be beaten by it. There is always work for people willing to put in the effort. Someone will always let you sleep on their sofa if they can see that you are serious about changing your life. As long as you are honest and have integrity most people will want to help you as much as they can. Recognise when you are being given a lucky break and make the very most of every opportunity.

The best thing about ditching bad habits is that it frees up space in our lives to form some good ones. Ultimately we want positive habits that boost our self-esteem and make us feel great, not habits we wish we didn't have hanging over our heads making us feel rubbish about ourselves.

We are what we eat

When I was growing up I ate a diet consisting mainly of processed junk. I was *that* kid scoffing chocolate and drinking coke on their way to school. Not knowing the first thing about cooking I ate budget ready-meals and fast food for years when I left home. After seeing the photos from my 21st birthday party, and being shocked by how much weight I'd put on, I knew it was time to change my eating habits.

It didn't happen overnight but during the next couple of years I taught myself how to cook, and moved towards cooking from scratch being the rule rather than the exception. Nowadays I create recipes and write about them on my blog. Good food is an integral part of my family's life; I love to cook and never see it as a chore. I view uninterrupted kitchen time as therapeutic and calming, something to truly look forward to.

Ask yourself whether you eat well or have fallen into bad habits with food? Do you cook from scratch or buy everything pre-prepared? Do you eat lots of sugary treats and processed carbohydrates? What we eat can have a huge effect over our entire wellbeing, and a diet consisting mainly of natural foods will provide energy, wake up a previously foggy brain and help us think straight. Once you get into good habits where food is concerned it quickly becomes second nature and you'll wonder why you haven't been eating this way all along. I have yet to meet a person that hasn't benefitted from cleaning up their diet.

I am not a qualified food expert; however, having been on both ends of the spectrum I feel that not knowing how to do something as important as cooking is not a good enough excuse. If you need inspiration it can be found everywhere by watching celebrity chefs, reading food blogs, watching YouTube videos and buying cookbooks. Local councils in the UK often have free cookery courses available to all, so it's worth checking out your council's website. If you're a complete beginner you will almost certainly have some kitchen disasters along the way, but don't be put off by them. As long as you learn from every single mistake you can put the knowledge to good use next time. As with anything else in life, persevere and you will get better.

If not having the time is what's stopping you then make the time by ditching the non-important things we discussed at the start of this chapter. Batch cooking and freezing is a fantastic way to ensure that you always have good food to hand without having to cook every day. You can pick up tin foil disposable containers from any supermarket. Set aside one afternoon every other weekend to be in the kitchen, make several large pots of food and freeze them into ready meals that can be pulled out whenever you need them. Choose easy recipes that will cause you the minimum amount of stress. Simple soups, stews and curries are a great place to start, and can be economical too, saving you a fortune in comparison to shop-bought equivalents.

A few tips for healthier eating

Fat burning: Get your body to burn fat for fuel instead of sugar by swapping the carbs at breakfast time for something more nutritious and substantial. When our body burns fat it stabilises our blood sugar levels which (among other things) means not getting hungry again so quickly. One of my favourite meals to start the day with is two scrambled eggs with half an avocado on the side. Why not try it and see how long it keeps you going for?

Snack swap: If you are quite partial to sugary treats and processed snacks in between meals, opt for more natural alternatives. Nutrient-dense foods such as organic nuts or plain live yoghurt will provide you with energy for longer.

Read carefully: Live by the rule 'the fewer ingredients the better'. Start scrutinising every single label of every item of food you buy that isn't in its natural state. Once you see how many unnecessary added ingredients are sneaked into processed food it is likely to be a massive turn-off.

Get moving

The 'happy' hormones (endorphins) that are released while exercising are a brilliant way to start feeling great about yourself. There are plenty of things you can do to gently kickstart getting fit, but you have to be disciplined. Set aside three time slots every week, at any time of the day that suits, solely for this purpose. Once it has become a good habit you'll find that it has blended into your weekly routine. Below are some suggestions of how to get started. Please ensure you always wear appropriate clothing and get the go-ahead from your GP before you start a new exercise programme.

Walking: Using your legs instead of the car or public transport is a great headstart to give yourself. It's completely free and kind to the planet; what's not to like? Also try taking the stairs instead of using the lift wherever possible.

Running: If you've always fancied running but never had the legs for it, search online for details on the 'Couch to 5k' running program. Running is a great way to get your endorphins flowing, and like walking costs zilch! The secret of the success of 'Couch to 5k' is its gentle introduction to getting started. When you first physically get off your couch you alternate between walking and running very small distances. This slowly builds up your capabilities and after eight weeks you will be able to run 5k or 30 minutes non-stop.

Cycling: If you already own a bike then use it. If you don't but quite like the idea of it then borrow one or pick up a second-hand bike to see if it's for you.

Going to the gym: Especially if you are able to access a subsidised membership, going to the gym is a great way of staying out of trouble. Make sure you actually use it and get your money's worth, though.

Classes: From yoga to Zumba, most local areas have sports and fitness classes run from leisure centres and halls. Some even offer a free taster session to see if you enjoy it. Make sure you are serious before signing up for a block of lessons, though, otherwise it will end up being a waste of money. Check out local directories for details. These classes are usually low cost and can be further reduced if you are studying or out of work.

Boot Camps: Many parks have 'boot camp' classes being run from them, usually by independent personal trainers. They are often not very expensive but they're great fun and can be really effective. Do a web search to find one near you.

DVDs at home: If you can find a DVD that you like then exercising at home is another great way of getting into shape. Once you've paid for the DVD it's completely free, and no-one else is around to watch. Search online to find the perfect workout for you.

Take up a sport: Whether you really enjoyed playing sports when you were younger, or want to take one up from scratch, connect with a local team and see if you can join them next time they train.

A few tips for your motivation

Extra time: If you're having an off day and feel you just can't be bothered try putting on your running/training/gym clothes and see how you feel then. Perhaps you just need a little extra time to warm up.

Friends: Team up with a group of friends and start your own boot camp in the park taking it in turns to lead the class. With the added incentive of not wanting to let the rest of the group down, you can keep each other motivated.

Variety: Give something new a go every now and then. If running is usually your thing, try a bit of yoga. If you take classes at the gym, try something different at home to see if you like it.

Other lifestyle changes

Losing weight: Nobody ever lost tons of weight by sitting around and talking about doing so. I believe the first step to losing weight has to be with looking at your diet and establishing good eating habits. In addition to this, regular exercise should ensure the weight starts coming off. Buy an outfit in your ideal size and use that as your motivator. It's also worth keeping a really unflattering photograph of yourself in a visible place. Once you start losing the weight you can look at the photo and remind yourself what you don't want to look like.

Smoking: A basic internet search will present you with the various techniques designed to help you give up smoking. Your GP will also be able to talk to you about local quitting programmes that are often completely free of charge. In addition to whichever one you choose, why not try putting the money you would have spent on cigarettes into a jar each day and reward yourself with a nice treat after six months? If you currently have a 20-a-day habit there will be a sizeable amount in that jar – maybe even enough for a little holiday somewhere.

Drinking: Speaking from experience, my drinking buddies were also people I had to disassociate myself from when I became serious about changing my life. Often these people are the reason we go out drinking or partying all weekend and end up spending the following week feeling like crap. By distancing yourself from the toxic people in your life you won't be going out with them and therefore won't spend the week feeling rubbish. Toxic relationships are just another form of bad habit to break; we will talk about them more in the next two chapters.

Giving up vices: If you have real addictions that are ruining your life then you will need to get specific help. As you are reading this book I'm going to trust that you want to change. Now you need to put everything you have learnt to good use and actually do some changing. Find a rehab centre, counsellor or group therapy session to suit your needs. Above all else, learn self-control.

Money troubles: If you are stuck in a financial rut, spending everything that you earn and then some, you will need to devise a strict budget and start living within your means. Think about the bigger picture and how the stuff you think you need makes you feel once it's been purchased. Needing something and wanting it are not the same. Learning to distinguish between our wants and our needs is a useful life skill to have. Once you are able to do so you will probably come to realise that you didn't *need* a lot of the things you originally thought you did. You just *wanted* them.

If you are in debt and concerned about paying back what you owe, speak with a free debt advisory service. They will be able to guide you through your options, and help you to formulate a debt management plan.

Hobbies: If you want to channel your energies productively then blogging can be a great hobby. It's completely free and can lead to endless opportunities. You could start a blog about becoming the best you. It could document your progress, acting as a fantastic keepsake to look back on and be proud of.

A suggested plan of action

Goals: Devise a set of personal goals that you would like to achieve, and get serious about making them happen. Remember to break them up into bite-sized manageable chunks, and keep your targets realistic. Think of a suitable reward to treat yourself with when you achieve your goals.

Cook: How long it will take you depends on your starting point, but over time learn how to cook good food from scratch. Once it is a regular habit it will start becoming easier.

Workout: Exercise regularly and get your endorphins flowing. Whether it's going for a short jog, taking a class or training in a gym, moving in any way is almost always better that not moving at all.

Please don't beat yourself up for the occasional calorific meal or a couple of missed work-outs, though. As long as it's not too often it is important to allow ourselves to have a blowout every now then. A little indulgence once in a while can serve as a great pick me up, especially if we're sharing the moment with loved ones.

Chapter Seven

REDEFINE THE RULES

"People come into your life for a reason, a season or a lifetime." *Anon.*

THE BEST example of successfully redefining the rules I can personally give comes from the period of time that my husband and I were giving our relationship 'one last try'. As I've already mentioned we had a very rocky year in Cambodia and came home to the UK separately. We quickly found jobs and flat-shares and started living life as singletons. Our future looked non-existent but neither of us were prepared to properly walk away. Without anything changing we started seeing each other again about two months after returning, and I moved in with him and his flatmates few months later.

By then we were already back to the old routine of drinking until all hours and partying hard at the weekend. I treated him horribly. We argued loads and I fought with his flatmates. It was an ugly time – one of the only periods of my life that I look back upon and feel utterly ashamed of. Within three months I'd decided enough was enough; we were to break up 'for good'. A few weeks after we went our separate ways I hit rock my rock bottom. This is when I woke up to myself and realised that I had thrown away the one person who truly loved me, and always had my best interests at heart.

I spent the next three months working hard on all the self-improvements I've spoken about here in this book, and was adamant to get back together with my then ex-boyfriend and make our relationship work. He was less enthusiastic. I had burnt him badly and he wasn't going to be as free and easy with his heart. If we were to give things one last try it would be on his terms; he would call the shots. If I was serious about making it work then I had to respect his wishes.

It turned out to be the best thing that happened to us, because I was no longer in control and able to make more bad decisions. Above all else, he said we had to take things slowly. We had been living together from the day we met, and he wanted us to remain living apart for the foreseeable future. We would only see each other at the weekend and concentrate on work and other commitments during the week. We would not waste our time drinking all night and being hungover. We would spend quality time together and do interesting things such as take trips out of London, visit exhibitions and go to nice restaurants.

The key to our success was that each of us wanted it to work out as much as the other. Within a few months we had redefined the rules of our relationship, and six months after getting back together we moved into our first home without flatmates. It was the making of us, and the rest as they say is history. There is absolutely no doubt in my mind that we would not have had a future together had both of us not been willing to change.

Examples of other relationships that need to have the rules redefined

Scenario: Your parents divorced while you were young and both remarried while you were in your teens. You get on well with one step-parent but have never particularly warmed to the other one and vice versa. Now that you are an adult they exclude you from family gatherings and you feel you don't get to see your parent as often as you would like.

Solution: If you want to have a better relationship one of you needs to be the bigger person and hold out the olive branch, so it might as well be you. If you want your parent to be an active part of your life it is vital that you get along with their partner. Start winning over your step-parent by being conciliatory and doing nice things for them. Invite them out to lunch or cook for them. Make it clear that you're sorry for your history and want to make it better by getting to know them. Be willing to accept responsibility for your part in the problem, and leave the ball in their court. Most people want to get on with their family and will relish the opportunity to make amends.

Scenario: Your relationship with a good friend has become very one-sided. You feel you are always doing the things they want to do, on their terms. You are always going out of your way for them, but they are nowhere to be seen when you could use some support.

Solution: It sounds like the other person is behaving quite selfishly. They genuinely might not have realised they have hurt you, so in the first instance try and talk to them about how you're feeling. If you want to continue with the friendship then start seeing them on your terms instead. Make it abundantly clear that you aren't going to only do the things they want to do anymore. If the other person doesn't co-operate then you might have to ask yourself whether the friendship is worth salvaging.

Scenario: You have become close to a work colleague and often go out socialising together. Secrets get divulged over drinks and this information could be used against each other to get ahead in the workplace.

Solution: Firstly it's important to always maintain your integrity by doing the right thing. As tempting as it might be, you must never use this type of information to further your own career. If you suspect the other person is doing so then ask them outright and see what they say. If trust has been lost then it's wise to stop drinking together, because leaving yourself so vulnerable when it comes to your professional life is too risky. If you feel you could have an 'outside work' friendship then go for coffee or lunch instead. It will be obvious pretty quickly whether this person is a friend or just a drinking buddy that you could do without while you are going through this process.

Choose your friends wisely

The best thing about friends and partners is that we get to pick who they are – unlike our family, where we have no say in the matter. I strongly believe that the people we meet on our journey through life help to determine our fortune along the way. As long as you have good people around enhancing your happiness, your life will always be a success in its own right. If we really are the average of the five people we spend the most time with, then you're unlikely to get very far by spending your days with people who sit in grotty basement flats smoking weed, eating junk food and playing computer games.

If you spend your time wisely, working on becoming the best possible you, then you'll attract good people into your world. To break the cycle it is absolutely imperative to surround yourself with the most fantastic people you can. They will help keep you on the straight and narrow when times get tough, and stand on the sidelines cheering you on when you need encouragement. Once you have established who the decent people in your life are – the true 'keepers' – ensure that your conscience is always clear by being a great friend to them. Listen attentively, never gossip and be a good secret-keeper. Do everything you can to keep hold of them because surrounding yourself with amazing people will help keep you on track. Having good influences around will also help you to recognise the bad influences that make your life harder work than it needs to be.

Have a look at the list below and remember that a genuinely good friend would never do any of these things:

- Gossip behind your back and share your secrets

- Steal your boy/girlfriend, money or possessions

- Encourage you to make bad choices

- Turn their back on you during a crisis

- Stir up trouble with other friends

- Intentionally set out to cause you pain

When partners bring you more heartache than happiness, family aren't being supportive, and 'friends' aren't being very friendly, it's advisable to put some distance between you. How much you miss them once they aren't around will be an indication of how long you need to stay away from them. We cannot change people, but we can change the way we interact with them in the hope that they realise the error of their ways and make necessary changes themselves. If they want a place in your life they need to earn it.

Assess your inner circle

We are going to carry out an exercise to pinpoint the people in your life who perhaps do not have your best interests at heart. Please ensure that you are alone, in a quiet peaceful place.

On an A4 sheet of paper write down all the people you frequently have in your life. List everybody from your parents to your partner, family members, friends and colleagues. Draw a line down the middle, write names on the left and leave the right side blank. Give yourself an inch of writing space per person.

- Now write down how each person made you feel the last three times you saw them:
  - Very happy
  - Happy
  - Indifferent
  - Sad
  - Miserable

- Now write down how much you argue with these people:
  - Every time you see them
  - Often
  - Occasionally
  - Never
- Now write down how much respect you have for them and their opinions:
  - Lots
  - Little
  - None

Faced with a result that looks like this:

- [insert name]:
  - Miserable
  - Often
  - None

can you really justify keeping them in your life as is?

Now reassess your inner circle

I don't know about you but over the years I have had numerous relationships with people that have made me miserable: family, friends, lovers, bosses, work colleagues. What I've learnt the hard way is that we cannot control another person's thoughts or actions. We do, however, have complete control over how we allow them to make us feel. If change needs to happen for your relationship to thrive then it's up to you both to do things differently.

Absence can make the heart grow fonder, so you may just need a little distance from the other person. Be completely transparent from the very start and explain to them that you need time to clear your head. It could be as little as a few days or as long as a few months. If they love you they should understand and be supportive. If they make your life difficult while you are going through this process their behaviour could answer the all-important question: Are they a keeper? If the answer is yes then it's imperative that you redefine the rules of your relationship by telling them that things cannot carry on as they are if you are to have a future together. It's not so much a set of rules, rather clear-cut boundaries. Here are some suggestions:

- See and speak to the other person on your terms. If they call you all the time, simply stop taking their calls and phone them back when it's convenient for you. Ditto texts, email and social media.

- If the other person is argumentative and picks a fight every time you see them, tell them that you aren't in the mood and have to leave the room.

Creating distance when things get overheated will allow you both to cool down.

- Start meeting on neutral territory. This means that you aren't always doing what the other person wants to do. It also means you can leave any time you want.

Say NO more often

Sometimes we need to push back a little in order to work out what we really want. Whether it's in a social capacity, the workplace or within your own family, saying 'no' is empowering. People often take advantage of those they know will say 'yes' to everything but rarely give them the respect they deserve. Working to anyone else's schedule but your own will make you feel miserable long-term, so start saying 'no'. There are many ways we can politely say 'no', while at the same time offering the other person a solution to the dilemma. Here are some examples:

- I'm so sorry but I can't come out tonight, I'm absolutely shattered after a hectic week at work. How about lunch on Sunday instead?

- I'm afraid I'm unable to lend you any more money. I am flat out broke! In fact I could really use you paying back what you already owe me.

- I won't be able to come over to your house this weekend; why don't you come to mine instead?

A suggested plan of action

Distance: If after assessing your inner circle you feel that some people do not have your best interests at heart, put some distance between the two of you. Ensure you are completely honest with the other person from the start; that way you will know that your conscience is clear and you haven't done anything wrong. It's only through secrets and lies that things become messy.

Slowly: If after your time apart you both want to try again then great, but take things slowly. Don't rush straight back to where you just were. Take your time and rediscover why you love this person and can't live without them.

Break: If after your time apart you feel the relationship does not have a future, consider a longer-term break from them. We will talk about toxic relationships in the next chapter.

Noteworthy

- Bullying in the workplace is completely unacceptable. If a colleague is making your life a misery then consider reporting them to Human Resources.

- You should never stay in a relationship that is damaging to your physical or emotional wellbeing.

If a partner, friend or family member is abusive in any way at all they should be reported to the appropriate authorities and dealt with accordingly.

Chapter Eight

CALL TIME ON TOXIC RELATIONSHIPS

"In the end only three things matter. How much you loved, how gently you lived, and how gracefully you let go of things not meant for you." *Buddha*

GETTING SOME distance can be a lot easier said than done. If you are in the unfortunate position of being surrounded by family who are draining your energy reserves then you need to do some serious thinking. Let's get one thing straight: being related to a person does not give them *carte blanche* to treat you badly. If you are going to break the cycle you will need to look long and hard at all your relationships and figure out who you are able to have in your life long-term. This is likely to be the most challenging part of the whole process, but it's where your new-found inner strength and self-respect will guide you to do the right thing.

Cutting ties with my mother was one of the toughest decisions I have ever had to make, but for the purposes of self-preservation I was left with no other choice.

When I tell people that I don't have her in my life, the first reaction I usually get is shock. Once I give them some details, however, they begin to understand why I did something that seems so drastic. In the end I had to ask myself, 'Will I be able to live the life I want (and deserve) with her still a part of it?' Sadly I concluded the answer was no.

Now that I'm a mum I can see how difficult her life must have been. Still a child herself she gave birth to me at 18 and had three kids by the age of 25, without the help of a supportive partner. Determined not to make all the mistakes her own mother made, she went ahead and made plenty of her own. For example, moving house – sometimes twice in the same year – to avoid paying debts meant that I went to eight schools. This played havoc with my self-confidence as well as my education.

She never thought her decisions through properly or considered the long-term consequences. Everything was done on a reactive level, only ever thinking of the moment she was in. This might be an acceptable way of living for a person without dependants, but as far as I'm concerned when you have children it is not good enough. When all is said and done, I have genuinely forgiven my mother for the things that I went through. I don't think she's a terrible person, and in spite of her numerous mistakes I honestly believe that she had the best interests of her children at heart most of the

time. Unfortunately she was young, foolish and naïve –
a disastrous combination.

When redefining the rules doesn't work

Forgiveness and respect are two very different beasts,
though, and I got to the point where I didn't like her
anymore. Counselling opened my eyes to how much
of a drain on my emotional resources she was and had
always been. I'd essentially been playing the parent role
to her irresponsible child for far too long and was fed up
of always coming to her rescue when she got herself into
trouble.

While I was going through counselling I tried my best
to redefine the rules of our relationship. I stopped
giving her money every time she got herself into a sticky
situation, and I stopped taking her phone calls while I
was at work. After initially resisting the new boundaries
she started respecting them. She soon realised that
it wasn't fair to view me as a never-ending source of
cash to be tapped whenever she found herself without
enough. That it wasn't fair to interrupt me when I was
at work to tell me her problems. I also started seeing
her less which helped immensely because when we did
spend time together I enjoyed her company much more
than I had been. By the time I left the UK to go travelling
we were in a good place and I was in email contact with
her while I was away.

Crunch time came shortly after going back to Cambodia to set up the shop. I was contacted by my half-brother and told that she had run off to Canada with a man she had met over the internet just a few months before. She had made yet another hasty decision that meant walking out of her life to start a new one, leaving behind a trail of destruction and debt in her wake. She stole electrical items from the place she worked, and took out a massive loan with one of her sisters with no intention of paying her half back. She left the flat she was renting with most of her belongings still in it, including every photograph from our childhood – memories that were captured long before the days of digital photography and completely irreplaceable.

The realisation dawned on me that over the course of the decade that followed my leaving home, I had lost all respect for her, and this was the final straw. In my heart of hearts I knew it was time to say goodbye to her for good because ultimately our relationship had become too toxic to save. That was almost ten years ago. To my knowledge she doesn't know that I am married, and she has never met her grandchildren. I have felt sadness over the years for the loss of what could have been but I have never once regretted my decision. Although I loved her, I could not allow her to bring her dramas to my life any longer.

Two choices

Some people are lucky enough to come from happy families. They don't harbour resentment towards their upbringing and they love their parents and siblings unconditionally. For those that aren't as fortunate it can be like navigating a minefield every time there is a family gathering. Rather than Christmas being a fun joyful occasion, it can end up being the very worst time of year – treading on eggshells and feeling responsible for other people's happiness.

When we are in the midst of a bad relationship we have two options available. We can try to change the other person, or we can change the way we interact with them. As we discussed in the previous chapter, distancing ourselves a little and redefining the rules can be extremely beneficial when a relationship has become toxic. Setting out new boundaries and changing our interaction can have a positive knock-on effect, which in turn prompts changes in the other person's behaviour. This is the best outcome we can hope for.

Sometimes even after we have exhausted our options and tried our very best, it still won't have sparked enough change in the other person. This is when you'll need to start considering your mental-health wellbeing, because no-one is worth you having a breakdown. If your emotional state is suffering because the other person is not willing to change, then I would suggest taking a huge step back from them. Time can often be the only true healer, and an extended break can be exactly what you both need to realise that your relationship is or isn't worth fighting for. What I personally had to learn the hardest way is that above all else self-preservation must come first. There is absolutely no point in being a martyr. You will not thank yourself for it in the long run.

Stay strong

When self-doubt washes over you, remember all the negative things that happened because of the other person. If you keep them in your life, will they destroy your confidence and leave you with no self-respect? Does their company hamper your ability to make good decisions and lead you down the path of mischief? Can you be the best you with them around? If their presence causes you nothing but upset, then they have left you with no other choice but to walk away. As long as you have been honest from the outset and maintained your integrity, your conscience should be completely clear.

If you do decide to cut people out of your life be prepared for the feelings of loss and sadness. If they were once an all-important part of your day to day then you will need to grieve over them. It's important to be extra gentle with yourself during this time and allow yourself these feelings. You might feel lonely and think you miss them terribly, but you must stay strong. Once you get through the initial difficulties you will soon realise how much better off you are without them. Now is the ideal time to start making all the positive changes that we have been talking about here in this book.

A suggested plan of action

Yes: Ask yourself: Can I live the life I want and deserve with them still a part of it? If the answer is yes then try to redefine the rules in the first instance. Ensure you conduct yourself with integrity at all times and have full faith in the decisions you are making.

No: If the answer is no or you try to redefine the rules but the other person is not willing to change, then self-preservation must prevail. You have been left with little choice but to exclude them from your life.

Walk away: If you do cut ties with people you must allow yourself to grieve over them. Time is often the best healer, and once the situation isn't so raw and painful you can revisit your options.

Chapter Nine

If You Don't Like It, Change It

"Yesterday is history. Tomorrow is a mystery.
Today is a gift – that's why it's called the present."
Kung Fu Panda

IN THIS recap chapter I have structured my advice
in the order that I feel is most relevant to helping you
move forward. Once I was serious about turning my
life around, it took me six months to implement all the
necessary changes I had to make to start becoming the
best me. Gradually over time the things I used to find
challenging became easier; nowadays I don't feel that it's
an effort to be a good person, or make good decisions –
they come naturally. I believe that absolutely anyone else
can do the same as long as they are 100% committed to
the cause.

Make peace with your past

- Get to the root of your troubles and tackle them head on. When you are ready to seek professional help do as much research as you can until you find the right method to suit your needs. Fully embrace the opportunity to get everything out in the open and place yourself on to the road to recovery. Do not hold back, this will be a vital part of your healing process.

- Forgive yourself for the things you have done because you can't go back in time and change history. Forgive those who have caused you pain and let go of hurt and anger over what has happened in the past. Once you become emotionally detached from your past it won't be able to rule your life anymore.

- Visit your happy place as often as you can and learn to control your thoughts so they do not end up controlling you.

During this time...

- Always be honest with yourself.

- Don't stress over the problems; instead, start thinking about the solutions.

Ensure that your glass is half full

- Start visualising the person you want to be and thinking about how you will become the best you.

- Devise a basic set of principles and start living by them every day. Self-reflect as often as possible and ensure that you learn from your mistakes by not repeating them.

- Do everything in your power to boost your confidence by doing things that make you feel good about yourself.

During this time...

- Look for the good in everything and everyone.

- Start truly believing in the power of YOU.

Go back to basics

- Get comfortable with spending time alone and enjoy your own company.

- Become interested in nature, and appreciate the beauty that can be found in the simplest of places.

- Eat well and enjoy all the benefits that a good clean diet will bring to your life.

During this time...

- Remember the phrase, 'the fewer ingredients the better'.

- Go for long walks when you need to clear your head.

Stop wasting your time

- If you are spending too much time on social networking sites then scale down your usage. Try my simple three-step plan in Chapter Five when you're ready to cut down.

- Ditch reality TV, tabloids and trashy magazines. Watch good quality TV and films on catch-up channels and streaming websites instead. Read about important world events through reputable news sites.

- Start thinking of hobbies and other ways that you could be using your spare time productively.

During this time...

- Remember that real friends will want to share their real lives with you.

- Remember that your time is a precious commodity. Spend it wisely by learning valuable life skills.

Ditch bad habits

- Carry out the exercise in Chapter Six and devise your list of personal goals. Keep your targets realistic ensuring they are high enough to count but low enough to attain.

- Work hard and set yourself apart from your colleagues. Keep your eye on the bigger picture and start thinking about your long-term career aspirations.

  - Ensure that by now you are eating a diet of good natural food and exercising regularly.

During this time...

- Don't be disheartened by rejection.

- Stay motivated by recognising your efforts and rewarding yourself along the way.

IF YOU DON'T LIKE IT, CHANGE IT

Assess (and reassess) your inner circle

- Carry out the exercise in Chapter Seven to assess your inner circle, and if you have people in your life that do not have your best interests at heart start reassessing it.

- If need be, try to redefine the rules of relationships with people that you want to keep in your life.

- If certain relationships have become too toxic to save, consider cutting ties for an extended period of time.

During this time...

- Do not let the takers take from you anymore.
- Allow yourself time to grieve over those you have excluded from your life.

Afterword

SOME CLOSING THOUGHTS

"The only impossible journey is the one you never begin." *Anthony Robbins*

I FEEL incredibly proud to have broken the cycle of dysfunction, and every single day I learn and grow, and work hard to ensure the cycle stays broken. I am truly grateful for this journey I've been through.

Being a parent is a huge responsibility that my husband and I take very seriously. We are often on the lookout for ways to improve our family's situation or help us through challenging times. We're always willing to take advice on-board and change direction if something isn't working.

It's up us to ensure that we equip our children with the necessary resources for them grow into well rounded young adults. Ultimately, all we can hope for is that our kids grow up happy and have fond memories of their childhood.